# WHOSE BABY ARE YOU?

Wendy Madgwick

Illustrated by John Francis

A caterpillar hatched from a tiny egg. It ate lots of leaves and got bigger and bigger. Then it turned into a brown cocoon. Inside the cocoon the caterpillar changes shape. Can you guess what it turns into?

It turns into a beautiful butterfly!

These baby birds live in the farmyard. Look at their big feet. They can walk well. But their wings are tiny. They cannot fly yet. Do you know whose babies they are?

The little birds are baby chicks. Their mother is a hen.

One day there was a tapping, cracking sound on the river bank. The big eggs were hatching! Can you see the little animals trying to break out of the eggs? Can you guess what they are?

Did you guess right?
These aren't birds. They
are baby crocodiles!

There are tadpoles in this pond. They hatched from the eggs. You can still see some eggs in the water. Soon the tadpoles will grow legs like their parents. Do you know what tadpoles grow into?

Tadpoles grow legs,
lose their tails and turn
into frogs. Croak!

These babies live in Africa. They play and fight together. They are learning how to hunt. Their mother is a good hunter. Their father has a fine golden mane. He is called the king of beasts. Do you know whose babies they are?